MONOLINGUAL

THE BASIC OXFORD

Picture Dictionary

Second Edition

MARGOT F. GRAMER

OXFORD

UNIVERSITY PRESS

OXFORD
UNIVERSITY PRESS

198 Madison Avenue
New York, NY 10016 USA

Great Clarendon Street
Oxford OX2 6DP England

Oxford New York
Auckland Bangkok Buenos Aires Cape Town Chennai
Dar es Salaam Delhi Hong Kong Istanbul Karachi Kolkata
Kuala Lumpur Madrid Melbourne Mexico City Mumbai Nairobi
São Paulo Shanghai Singapore Taipei Tokyo Toronto

with an associated company in *Berlin*

OXFORD is a trademark of Oxford University Press.

ISBN 0-19-437232-4

Copyright © 2003 Oxford University Press

Library of Congress Cataloging-in-Publication Data
Gramer, Margot.
    The basic Oxford picture dictionary / Margot F. Gramer; illustrations
    by Wendy Wassink Ackison . . . [et al.].—Monolingual / 2nd ed.
       p. cm.
    Includes index.
    ISBN 0-19-437232-4
    1. Picture dictionaries, English.   I. Title
    PE1629.G68 2003   423'.1—dc21   2002016955

Illustrations by: Wendy Wassink Ackison, Skip Baker,
Mary Chandler, Steven Chorney, Graphic Chart & Map Co.,
International Mapping Associates, Karen Loccisano,
Laura Hartman Maestro, Yoshi Miyake, Rob Schuster,
Joel Snyder, Gary Undercuffler, Anna Veltfort

Icons by Stephan Van Litsenborg

Editorial Manager: Janet Aitchison
Project Manager: Amy Cooper
Senior Production Editor: Jeff Holt
Production Editor: Stephanie Ruiz
Design Project Manager: Mary Chandler
Designer: Jennifer Manzelli
Senior Art Buyer: Jodi Waxman
Production Manager: Shanta Persaud
Production Coordinator: Eve Wong

Cover Concept: Silver Editions
Cover Illustrations by: Craig Attebery, Skip Baker, Jim DeLapine,
Narda Lebo, Mohammad Mansoor, Tom Newsom

Printing (last digit): 10 9 8 7 6 5 4 3 2 1

Printed in Hong Kong.

Acknowledgements

Oxford University Press gratefully acknowledges the work of the teachers and administrators who helped to shape this book:

Jayme Adelson-Goldstein, Los Angeles Unified School District

Fiona Armstrong, New York City Board of Education

Shirley Brod, Spring Institute for International Studies

Ann Creighton, Los Angeles Unified School District

Irene Frankel, The New School for Social Research

Rheta Goldman, North Hollywood Adult Learning Center

Jean Pilger, New York City Board of Education

Norma Shapiro, Los Angeles Unified School District

Kathleen Santopietro Weddel, Consultant, Northern Colorado State Literacy Resource Center

Renée Weiss, North Hollywood Adult Learning Center

Our special thanks to Jayme Adelson-Goldstein, Fiona Armstrong, and Norma Shapiro, who served as *Dictionary* consultants and wrote the accompanying *Teacher's Resource Book of Reproducible Activities, Workbook,* and *Picture Cards.* Ms. Adelson-Goldstein and Ms. Shapiro also wrote the *Teacher's Book.* The deep commitment of the authors to student-centered learning played a critical role in the development of *The Basic Oxford Picture Dictionary Program.*

To the Teacher

The Basic Oxford Picture Dictionary Program

Developed specifically to meet the needs of low-beginning adult and young adult students, including literacy-level learners, *The Basic Oxford Picture Dictionary Program* is a flexible four-skills course that addresses the critical language needs of beginning ESL and EFL students. *The Basic Oxford Picture Dictionary,* the core of the program, provides a rich, clear visual presentation of key vocabulary in meaningful contexts—language that is essential for the development of the beginning learner's survival skills. Used alone, the *Dictionary* is an invaluable resource. Together with its components, the *Dictionary Cassettes, Teacher's Book, Teacher's Resource Book of Reproducible Activities* and *Cassette, Workbook, Picture Cards, Transparencies,* and *Literacy Program,* it forms a comprehensive language development program.

The Basic Oxford Picture Dictionary, Second Edition

The Basic Oxford Picture Dictionary, Second Edition has several new important features that make the *Dictionary* even more useful and accessible to beginning students and their teachers:

- Easy exercises on every topic give students immediate practice with the new vocabulary.

- A color-coded guide enables students and teachers to locate units by topic more easily.

- Some artwork has been revised to reflect a more contemporary style.

- A new *Teacher's Book* includes the complete *Basic Oxford Picture Dictionary, Second Edition* within it. Wrap-around notes offer step-by-step lesson plans, teaching strategies, creative ideas for lesson expansion, and cultural notes.

It is important to note that *The Basic Oxford Picture Dictionary, Second Edition* still has the same key features that have made the original edition of the *Dictionary* so popular: clear page design, large, easy-to-read type, and a limited number of words per page. The 1,200 high-frequency words and phrases—vocabulary that is most relevant to the everyday experience of adult and young adult learners—remain the same as in the previous edition. Vocabulary is presented in full-color illustrations, which depict each entry in its real-life context. The *Dictionary* is divided into 12 distinct thematic areas; however, pages may be used at random, depending on students' particular needs.

The most common name for any given item is used for simplicity. (When two names for an item exist, both are often included.) Nouns, adjectives, and prepositions are identified by number; verbs are identified by letter. In addition, illustrations are consecutively numbered, left to right, and top to bottom, wherever possible.

An index and pronunciation guide in the Appendix help students and teachers locate words and their correct pronunciations quickly. A complete set of *Dictionary Cassettes* offers a reading of all the words in the *Dictionary.*

Using *The Basic Oxford Picture Dictionary, Second Edition* Effectively

The Basic Oxford Picture Dictionary is an ideal resource for low-beginning and pre-literate students. The suggestions below are designed to provide a framework for using *The Basic Oxford Picture Dictionary* effectively within a communicative lesson. For further teaching suggestions, see *The Basic Oxford Picture Dictionary Teacher's Book* and the *Teacher's Resource Book of Reproducible Activities.*

1. Select a topic that meets your students' needs.

The 68 different topics shown in the *Dictionary*'s Contents pages reflect beginning students' crucial language needs. When selecting a particular topic to teach, consider your class's course outline as well as your students' immediate needs. You may want to involve your students by having them look at the Table of Contents and name the topics that interest them. Topics are grouped into 12 thematic areas, but you can recombine pages into units or themes appropriate for your particular group. For example, you might choose Vegetables, page 34, Cooking a Meal, page 46, and A Birthday Party, page 17, to create a lesson on preparing a meal for a special occasion.

2. Introduce the topic.

Have students look at the selected *Dictionary* page or the corresponding *Overhead Transparency.* Before students practice saying the new word, it is helpful to relate the topic to the students' lives and to let them hear the words in the context of words they already know. You may want to ask students to look at the page and point out words that they are already familiar with. Students could also brainstorm other words they know about the topic. In addition, you could describe the picture very simply, using some of the words students know, and then ask questions. For example, to introduce page 25: *This is a kitchen. There's a woman in the kitchen. She's opening the freezer. What do you think she's taking out of the freezer? What do you think she's making?* and so on. Using facial expression and gesture can help convey meaning. Since many of the pages of the *Dictionary* include people, you could ask the students to think about what the people might be doing.

3. Present the words on the page.

Once you've discovered which words your students already know, you can focus on the remaining ones. One way to present the words is to point to the picture while pronouncing the word. The students can follow along, looking at each picture in their books as you repeat the process for all the words. After students make the connection between the spoken word and picture, they can look at the written word, as you read each one. In this way, students will learn to associate the sound of the word with the picture, as well as with the written word.

After the initial presentation, you can say a word at random and have students point to the appropriate picture. To check comprehension, you may want to walk around the room as you speak to monitor responses. Then you can do the reverse—point (or have a student volunteer point) to a picture and have the students say the corresponding word. You can also check understanding by introducing question forms, such as *What is number 3?* or *What number is mop?*

4. Practice the words.

The exercises at the bottom of the page will reinforce the sound/word correspondences and the meaning of the words as students practice the target vocabulary in natural contexts. To support their practice, it is a good idea to model the language in each exercise before students begin. Examples on every page show them how to use the new words and phrases. All of the underlined words in the examples can be replaced with other words on the *Dictionary* page. By performing these substitutions, students practice the vocabulary on each page thoroughly.

Exercises

• Name or Talk about. . . . Point.

The first exercise on each page usually requires either a simple identification, e.g., *This is a pencil,* or a description, e.g., *There's an armchair, She's wearing a dress.* Students say the sentence and point to the corresponding picture in the *Dictionary.* In some cases, students are asked to count various items in the picture. In all of these activities, different structures are modeled in the examples and use the most context-appropriate, natural language for the target vocabulary.

• Ask and answer questions.

There are several variations of this activity throughout the text. In all of them, students ask and answer questions about the pictures on the page. These are paired activities, which divide the task into A and B dialogue roles. The exercises can be done in pairs of students or as a whole class, with half the class taking the part of A and the other half, the part of B.

• Act it out.

There are also a few variations of this TPR activity included in the exercises. In these activities, students act out vocabulary items for each other and guess the words. *Act it out* exercises can be done either in pairs or with the whole class.

• Talk about yourself.

Many pages include this final exercise, which gives the students an opportunity to relate the vocabulary to their own lives. It is often a paired activity, which can also be done in small groups.

Language notes

Several *Dictionary* pages include language notes, which provide additional guidance that may be needed to elicit natural language using the target vocabulary. The notes generally include article usage, plural forms, and various verb forms (past tense, present continuous, and third-person simple present forms).

5. Provide more practice.

There are numerous suggestions for communicative practice in both *The Basic Oxford Picture Dictionary Teachers' Book* and the *Teacher's Resource Book of Reproducible Activities.* Both offer activities based on *Dictionary* topics and are designed to improve students' listening, speaking, reading, writing, and cooperative skills. *The Basic Oxford Picture Dictionary Workbook* presents new contexts for the vocabulary in short reading and writing exercises.

6. Select an application activity.

Once students are familiar with the words on a page or within a unit, it is important to encourage them to apply this knowledge to the real world outside the classroom. Some activities you may want to try are:

- Have students look through magazines, newspapers, and other periodicals to find pictures of the topic of focus.

- Ask students to interview someone outside of the class (a family member or a friend), using questions that incorporate the new vocabulary.

- Assign the starred application activities in *The Basic Oxford Picture Dictionary Workbook* as homework and discuss the responses in class the next day.

Contents

5. The Market

6. Meal Time

7. Clothes

8. Health

1. (chalk)board *pizarron*
2. chalk *yeso*
3. eraser *borar*
4. teacher
5. student
6. chair
7. desk

8. book
9. paper
10. pen
11. pencil
12. notebook
13. computer

Language note:

a chalkboard
an eraser
a piece of chalk
a piece of paper

Name the things in the classroom. Point.

This is a pencil.
This is an eraser.

A. write	**H.** look at the screen *pantalla*
B. point (to) *apuntar*	**I.** close the window
C. go out	**J.** open a notebook
D. come in	**K.** raise . . . hand
E. read	**L.** talk
F. listen	**M.** sit
G. work at the computer	**N.** stand

A: Tell your partner what to do.
B: Act it out.
A: Please <u>raise your hand</u>.
Please <u>stand</u>.

JAN. ①						
Sun.	Mon.	Tue.	Wed.	Thurs.	Fri.	Sat.
					1	2
3	4	5	6	7	8	9
10	11	12	13	14	15	16
17	18	19	20	21	22	23
24/31	25	26	27	28	29	30

FEB. ②						
Sun.	Mon.	Tue.	Wed.	Thurs.	Fri.	Sat.
	1	2	3	4	5	6
7	8	9	10	11	12	13
14	15	16	17	18	19	20
21	22	23	24	25	26	27
28						

MAR. ③						
Sun.	Mon.	Tue.	Wed.	Thurs.	Fri.	Sat.
	1	2	3	4	5	6
7	8	9	10	11	12	13
14	15	16	17	18	19	20
21	22	23	24	25	26	27
28	29	30	31			

APR. ④						
Sun.	Mon.	Tue.	Wed.	Thurs.	Fri.	Sat.
				1	2	3
4	5	6	7	8	9	10
11	12	13	14	15	16	17
18	19	20	21	22	23	24
25	26	27	28	29	30	

MAY ⑤						
Sun.	Mon.	Tue.	Wed.	Thurs.	Fri.	Sat.
						1
2	3	4	5	6	7	8
9	10	11	12	13	14	15
16	17	18	19	20	21	22
23/30	24/31	25	26	27	28	29

JUNE ⑥						
Sun.	Mon.	Tue.	Wed.	Thurs.	Fri.	Sat.
		1	2	3	4	5
6	7	8	9	10	11	12
13	14	15	16	17	18	19
20	21	22	23	24	25	26
27	28	29	30			

JULY ⑦						
Sun.	Mon.	Tue.	Wed.	Thurs.	Fri.	Sat.
				1	2	3
4	5	6	7	8	9	10
11	12	13	14	15	16	17
18	19	20	21	22	23	24
25	26	27	28	29	30	31

AUG. ⑧						
Sun.	Mon.	Tue.	Wed.	Thurs.	Fri.	Sat.
1	2	3	4	5	6	7
8	9	10	11	12	13	14
15	16	17	18	19	20	21
22	23	24	25	26	27	28
29	30	31				

SEPT. ⑨						
Sun.	Mon.	Tue.	Wed.	Thurs.	Fri.	Sat.
			1	2	3	4
5	6	7	8	9	10	11
12	13	14	15	16	17	18
19	20	21	22	23	24	25
26	27	28	29	30		

OCT. ⑩						
Sun.	Mon.	Tue.	Wed.	Thurs.	Fri.	Sat.
					1	2
3	4	5	6	7	8	9
10	11	12	13	14	15	16
17	18	19	20	21	22	23
24/31	25	26	27	28	29	30

NOV. ⑪						
Sun.	Mon.	Tue.	Wed.	Thurs.	Fri.	Sat.
	1	2	3	4	5	6
7	8	9	10	11	12	13
14	15	16	17	18	19	20
21	22	23	24	25	26	27
28	29	30				

DEC. ⑫						
Sun.	Mon.	Tue.	Wed.	Thurs.	Fri.	Sat.
			1	2	3	4
5	6	7	8	9	10	11
12	13	14	15	16	17	18
19	20	21	22	23	24	25
26	27	28	29	30	31	

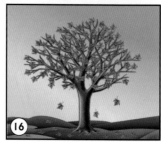

13 14 15 16

1. January
2. February
3. March
4. April
5. May
6. June
7. July
8. August

9. September
10. October
11. November
12. December
13. winter
14. spring
15. summer
16. fall

Talk about the months and seasons. Point.
This is January. It's winter.

Talk about yourself.
A: *Do you like winter?*
B: *Yes, I do. / No, I don't.*

JANUARY

① Sun.	② Mon.	③ Tue.	④ Wed.	⑤ Thurs.	⑥ Fri.	⑦ Sat.
					⑧ 1	⑨ 2
⑩ 3	4	5	6	7	8	9
10	11	12	13	⑭ 14	15	16
17	18	19	⑮ 20	21	22	23
24/31	25	26	27	28	29	30

⑯

JAN.	FEB.	MAR.

JAN.

Sun.	Mon.	Tue.	Wed.	Thurs.	Fri.	Sat.
					1	2
3	4	5	6	7	8	9
10	11	12	13	14	15	16
17	18	19	20	21	22	23
24/31	25	26	27	28	29	30

FEB.

Sun.	Mon.	Tue.	Wed.	Thurs.	Fri.	Sat.
	1	2	3	4	5	6
7	8	9	10	11	12	13
14	15	16	17	18	19	20
21	22	23	24	25	26	27
28						

MAR.

Sun.	Mon.	Tue.	Wed.	Thurs.	Fri.	Sat.
	1	2	3	4	5	6
7	8	9	10	11	12	13
14	15	16	17	18	19	20
21	22	23	24	25	26	27
28	29	30	31			

APR.

Sun.	Mon.	Tue.	Wed.	Thurs.	Fri.	Sat.
				1	2	3
4	5	6	7	8	9	10
11	12	13	14	15	16	17
18	19	20	21	22	23	24
25	26	27	28	29	30	

MAY

Sun.	Mon.	Tue.	Wed.	Thurs.	Fri.	Sat.
						1
2	3	4	5	6	7	8
9	10	11	12	13	14	15
16	17	18	19	20	21	22
23/30	24/31	25	26	27	28	29

JUNE

Sun.	Mon.	Tue.	Wed.	Thurs.	Fri.	Sat.
		1	2	3	4	5
6	7	8	9	10	11	12
13	14	15	16	17	18	19
20	21	22	23	24	25	26
27	28	29	30			

JULY

Sun.	Mon.	Tue.	Wed.	Thurs.	Fri.	Sat.
				1	2	3
4	5	6	7	8	9	10
11	12	13	14	15	16	17
18	19	20	21	22	23	24
25	26	27	28	29	30	31

AUG.

Sun.	Mon.	Tue.	Wed.	Thurs.	Fri.	Sat.
1	2	3	4	5	6	7
8	9	10	11	12	13	14
15	16	17	18	19	20	21
22	23	24	25	26	27	28
29	30	31				

SEPT.

Sun.	Mon.	Tue.	Wed.	Thurs.	Fri.	Sat.
			1	2	3	4
5	6	7	8	9	10	11
12	13	14	15	16	17	18
19	20	21	22	23	24	25
26	27	28	29	30		

OCT.

Sun.	Mon.	Tue.	Wed.	Thurs.	Fri.	Sat.
					1	2
3	4	5	6	7	8	9
10	11	12	13	14	15	16
17	18	19	20	21	22	23
24/31	25	26	27	28	29	30

NOV.

Sun.	Mon.	Tue.	Wed.	Thurs.	Fri.	Sat.
	1	2	3	4	5	6
7	8	9	10	11	12	13
14	15	16	17	18	19	20
21	22	23	24	25	26	27
28	29	30				

DEC.

Sun.	Mon.	Tue.	Wed.	Thurs.	Fri.	Sat.
			1	2	3	4
5	6	7	8	9	10	11
12	13	14	15	16	17	18
19	20	21	22	23	24	25
26	27	28	29	30	31	

1. Sunday
2. Monday
3. Tuesday
4. Wednesday
5. Thursday
6. Friday
7. Saturday
8. 1st

9. 2nd
10. 3rd
11. yesterday
12. today
13. tomorrow
14. day
15. week
16. year

Talk about the calendar.

Today is Wednesday.
Tomorrow is _____.
Yesterday was _____.

Talk about this week. Use words 1–7.

Today is _____.
Tomorrow is _____.
Yesterday was _____.

1. morning
2. afternoon *medio dia*
3. evening *tarde*
4. night

5. sun
6. moon
7. stars

Talk about pictures 1–4. Point.
It's morning.

A: **Ask questions.**
B: **Act out the answers.**
A: *What do you do in the morning?*
   What do you do at night?

6

1. clock
2. noon   *medio día*
3. midnight *media noche*
4. ten o'clock

5. ten fifteen
6. ten thirty
7. ten forty-five

Talk about the time. Point.

It's ten o'clock.

A: Ask the question and point.
B: Answer.

A: What time is it?
B: It's 9:30.

Look at page 6, pictures 1 and 3.
A: Ask questions and point.
B: Answer.

A: Is it 7:00 A.M. or 7:00 P.M.?
B: It's _____.

7

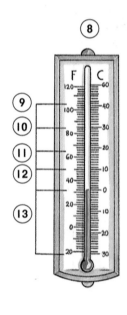

1. raining *lluvia*
2. snowing *nieve*
3. windy *con viento*
4. sunny *soleado*
5. cloudy *nublado*
6. icy
7. foggy *neblina*

8. temperature *termometro*
9. hot *caliente*
10. warm *tibio*
11. cool
12. cold *frio*
13. freezing *muy frio*

Talk about pictures 1–7. Point.

It's <u>raining</u>.

Language note:

° = degrees; F = Fahrenheit; C = Celsius
32°F = 0°C = freezing

Ask and answer questions.

A: *How's the weather?*
B: *It's <u>sunny</u> and <u>warm</u>.*
A: *What's the temperature?*
B: *It's <u>82°F</u> / <u>28°C</u>.*

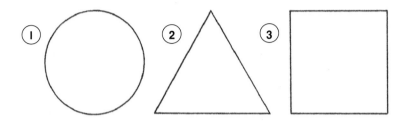

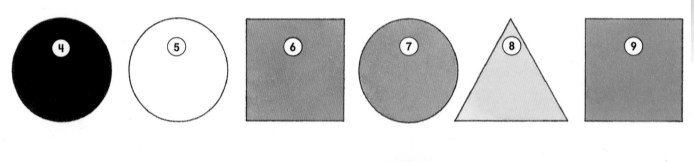

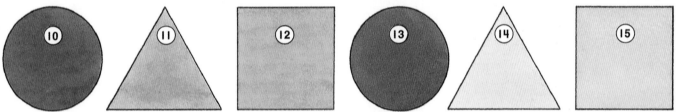

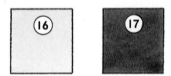

1. circle
2. triangle
3. square
4. black
5. white
6. red
7. blue
8. yellow
9. green

10. brown
11. gray
12. orange
13. purple
14. beige
15. pink
16. light (blue)
17. dark (blue)

Name the shapes and colors. Point.

This is a white circle.
This is an orange square.

Talk about yourself.

A: *What colors do you like?*
B: *I like _____ and _____.*

1. bills *billete*
2. dollar
3. coins *monedas todas*
4. penny *centavo*
5. nickel *5*
6. dime *10*
7. quarter *25*
8. cents
9. check *cuenta*
10. bill *cobro*
11. receipt *recivo*
12. credit card

Name the bills and coins. Point.
Use pictures 2, 4–7.

This is a dollar.
This is a penny.

Language note:

1 nickel	2 nickels
1 penny	2 pennies

Talk about yourself.

I have a quarter and two dimes.

1. baby	**5.** man
2. girl	**6.** child
3. boy	**7.** teenager *adolecente*
4. woman	**8.** adult

Talk about the people. Point.

She's a baby.
He's a boy.

Use the new words with pages 20–21.
A: Ask questions and point.
B: Answer.
A: *Is she a teenager?*
B: *Yes, she is.* / *No, she's an adult.*

11

Describing People

Height

1. tall
2. average height   *normal*
3. short

Weight

4. heavy / fat   *vien gordo*
5. average weight
6. thin / skinny

Size

7. big / large
8. small / little

Talk about the people. Point.

She's <u>tall</u>.
He's <u>heavy</u>.

A: Ask questions and point.
B: Answer.

A: *What does <u>she</u> look like?*
B: *<u>She's small, short, and thin</u>.*

Hair

9. beard
10. mustache
11. long hair
12. short hair
13. bald
14. straight hair
15. wavy hair
16. curly hair

17. blond hair
18. red hair
19. brown hair
20. black hair
21. gray hair

Age

22. young
23. middle-aged
24. old

Talk about the people. Point.

He has a beard.
She has long hair.
He's bald.
She's young.

13

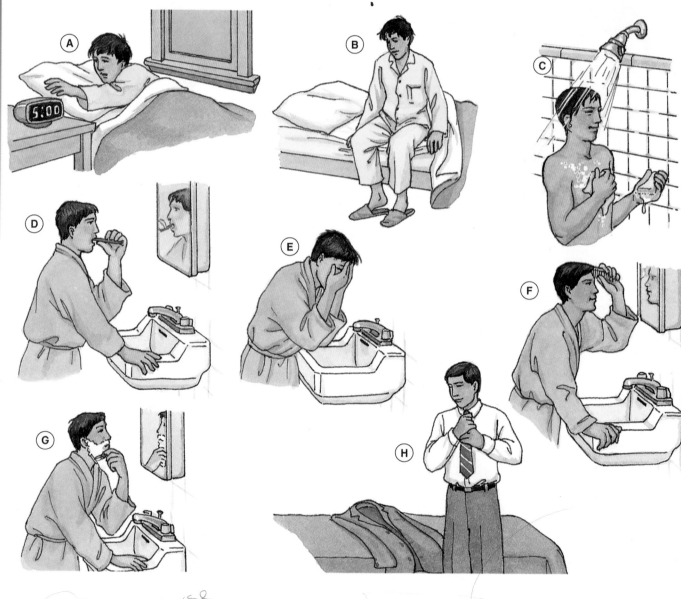

A. wake up   *despertarse*
B. get up   *levantar*
C. take a shower   *tomar un baño*
D. brush . . . teeth

E. wash . . . face
F. comb . . . hair
G. shave
H. get dressed

Language note:

wake up	→	*wakes up*
get up	→	*gets up*
brush . . . teeth	→	*brushes teeth*

Talk about the pictures. Point.

First, he gets up.
Then, he takes a shower.
Next, he brushes his teeth.

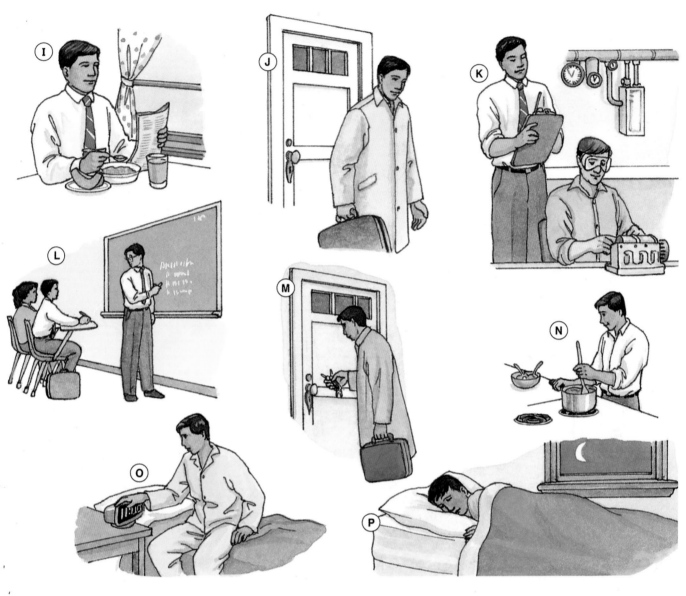

I. eat breakfast *desayunar*

J. leave the house

K. work *trabajar*

L. study/learn *estudiar*

M. come home *entrar a casas*

N. cook dinner *cocinar la cena*

O. go to bed *ir a la cama*

P. go to sleep *ir a dormir*

Ask and answer questions.
Use pictures I, K, L, N.

A: Do you <u>eat breakfast</u> every day?

B: Yes, I do. / No, I don't.

Talk about yourself.

First, I <u>get dressed</u>.

Then, I _____.

Next, I _____.

1. grandparents Abuelos
2. father papa
3. mother mama
4. sister hermana
5. brother hermano.
6. uncle tio
7. aunt Tia.
8. cousins Sobrinos

9. husband Esposo
10. wife Esposa.
11. parents
12. son
13. daughter
14. niece
15. nephew

Talk about the little boy's family.
Use pictures 1–8.

He has a sister.
He has an uncle.
He has grandparents.

Talk about your family.

I have a son and a daughter.

A. give a present to	**F.** blow out the candles
B. laugh	**G.** take a picture
C. kiss	**H.** drink milk
D. smile	**I.** cut the cake
E. sing	**J.** open a card

Language note:

give → giving
laugh → laughing
cut → cutting

Talk about the picture. Point.

She's giving a present to the boy.
He's laughing.
He's kissing the baby.

1. angry Enojada
2. happy felic
3. sad Triste
4. nervous

5. bored Aburido.
6. scared
7. excited

Talk about the people. Point.

She's angry.
He's happy.
They're scared.

A: **Ask questions.**
B: **Answer and point.**
A: *Who's embarrassed?*
B: *He is.*

8. surprised
9. worried
10. tired
11. hungry *Hambriento*

12. thirsty *sediento*
13. embarrassed
14. homesick

A: **Tell your partner how to act.**
B: **Act it out.**
A: *You're sad.*

Talk about your feelings.
I'm nervous today.
I'm tired today.

A. be born Recien nacido
B. start school Entrar a la escuela
C. graduate graduarse.

D. get a job trabajar
E. retire retirarse.

Language note:

Today		In the past
be born	→	was born
start	→	started
graduate	→	graduated
get	→	got
fall	→	fell
have	→	had

Talk about the pictures. Point.
She was born in 1990.
He moved.
They got married.

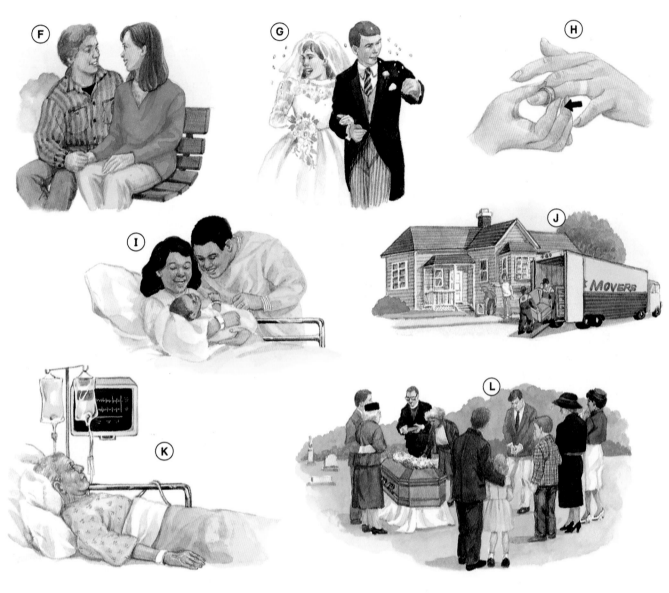

F. fall in love

G. get married *casarse*

H. get divorced *divorsiarse*

I. have a baby *tener un bebe*

J. move *modarse*

K. get sick *enfermarse*

L. die *morir*

Talk about your life.

A: When did you <u>start school</u>?

B: In <u>1998</u>.

A: When did you <u>get married</u>?

B: In <u>2000</u>.

A: When did you <u>move to the U.S.</u>?

B: In <u>1998</u>.

1. chimney
2. roof
3. porch ایوان
4. front door
5. window
6. garage
7. driveway راه ماشین

8. lawn
9. garbage can
10. deck
11. patio
12. backyard
13. garden

Talk about the house at the top.

The house has <u>a porch</u>.
It doesn't have <u>a deck</u>.

Talk about the house at the bottom.

The house has <u>a patio</u>.
It doesn't have <u>a garage</u>.

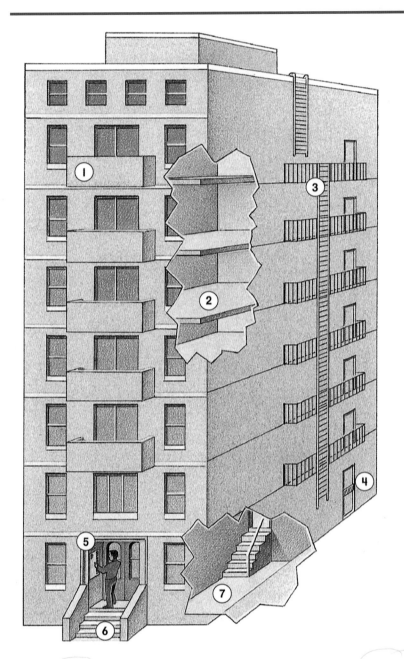

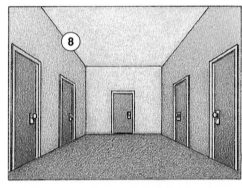

1. balcony
2. floor
3. fire escape
4. (fire) exit
5. entrance
6. steps
7. basement

8. hall
9. lobby
10. elevator
11. mailboxes
12. stairway/stairs
13. intercom

Talk about the apartment building.
A: Ask questions.
B: Answer and point.

A: *Where's the balcony?*
B: *Here it is.*

A: *Where are the steps?*
B: *Here they are.*

Talk about your home.

A: *Do you live in an apartment or a house?*
B: *I live in a house. What about you?*

23

1. ceiling *Techo*	**8.** end table
2. wall *Pared*	**9.** coffee table
3. floor *Piso*	**10.** rug
4. drapes	**11.** couch/sofa *sofa*
5. armchair/easy chair	**12.** bookcase *librero*
6. lamp *lampara*	**13.** stereo (system) *esterio*
7. (tele)phone *telefono*	**14.** television/TV *Television*

Talk about the living room. Point.

There's an armchair.
There's a lamp.
There are drapes.

Talk about your living room.

I have a couch in my living room.
I have two rugs, too.

1. microwave (oven)
2. pot
3. (tea)kettle
4. burner
5. skillet/(frying) pan
6. stove/range
7. oven
8. broiler

9. can opener
10. kitchen sink
11. trash can
12. cabinet
13. toaster
14. counter
15. freezer
16. refrigerator

Talk about the kitchen.

A: **Ask questions.**

B: **Answer and point.**

A: *Where's the microwave?*

B: *Here it is.*

Talk about your kitchen.

I have an oven, a _____ , and a _____ .

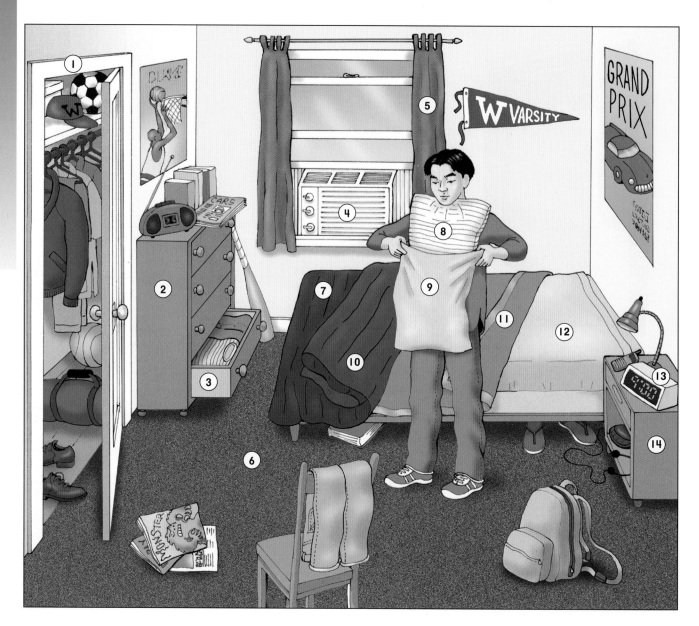

1. closet
2. dresser/bureau
3. drawer
4. air conditioner
5. curtains
6. carpet
7. bed

8. pillow
9. pillowcase
10. bedspread
11. blanket
12. sheets
13. alarm clock
14. night table

Talk about the bedroom. Point.
There's a closet.
There are curtains.

Name four things you use on a bed.

Talk about your bedroom.
I have an alarm clock and a dresser.
I have two beds.

1. shower دوش
2. shower curtain پرده حمام
3. faucet شیر آب
4. drain لوله فاضلاب
5. bathtub
6. wastebasket
7. sink

8. mirror
9. medicine chest /
   medicine cabinet
10. hamper سبد رخت
    چرکها
11. towel
12. toilet
13. toilet paper

Talk about the bathroom. Point.

There's a shower.
There's toilet paper.

A: **Ask the question and point.**
B: **Answer.**
A: *What's this?*
B: *A drain.*

27

A. make the bed

B. pick up/straighten up
   the room

C. clean the bathroom

D. vacuum the rug

E. dust the furniture

F. wash the dishes

G. dry the dishes

H. water the plants

I. rake the leaves

J. take out the garbage

Language note:

make → making
pick up → picking up
mop → mopping

Talk about the picture. Point.

She's <u>making the bed</u>.
They're <u>straightening up the room</u>.
He's <u>cleaning the bathroom</u>.

K. empty the wastebasket

L. change the sheets

M. sweep the floor

N. wash the windows

O. mop the floor

P. do the laundry

Q. plant a tree

R. mow the lawn

A: Ask questions and point.

B: Answer.

A: *What's he doing?*

B: *He's emptying the wastebasket.*

A: Ask the question. Act it out.

B: Guess.

A: *What am I doing?*

B: *You're mowing the lawn.*

Talk about your housework.

I wash the dishes and do the laundry.

1. mop
2. broom
3. dustpan
4. vacuum cleaner
5. cloth/rag
6. cleanser

7. rubber gloves
8. (scrub) brush
9. sponge
10. paper towels
11. bucket
12. outlet

Talk about the picture.

A: Ask questions.

B: Answer and point.

A: *Where's the mop?*

B: *Here it is.*

A: *Where are the paper towels?*

B: *Here they are.*

Talk about yourself.

A: *What do you use to clean?*

B: *I use a sponge and rubber gloves.*

1. pliers
2. wrench
3. screwdriver
4. hammer
5. saw
6. drill
7. tape measure
8. flashlight

9. toolbox
10. (step)ladder
11. hose
12. rake
13. shovel
14. lawn mower
15. nail
16. screw

Name the tools. Point.

These are pliers.
This is a wrench.

A: Ask the question. Act it out.
B: Guess.
A: What am I using?
B: A rake.

1. leaking roof / ceiling
2. cracked wall
3. broken window
4. cracked ceiling

5. no heat
6. stopped-up toilet
7. no hot water
8. broken lock

Talk about the problems. Point.

There's a leaking roof.
There's no heat.
There are cockroaches.
The refrigerator's not working.

A: Ask the question and point.
B: Answer.

A: *What's the problem?*
B: *There's a cracked wall.*

9. broken steps
10. dripping faucet
11. clogged drain
12. refrigerator not working

13. (cock)roaches
14. mice
15. flooded basement

Language note:

a leaking roof	*The roof is leaking.*
a broken lock	*The lock is broken.*
a clogged drain	*The drain is clogged.*

Look at pictures 1–4, 6, 8–11, 15.
Ask and answer questions.

A: *What's wrong with <u>the ceiling</u>?*
B: *It's <u>leaking</u>.*
A: *What's wrong with <u>the steps</u>?*
B: *They're <u>broken</u>.*

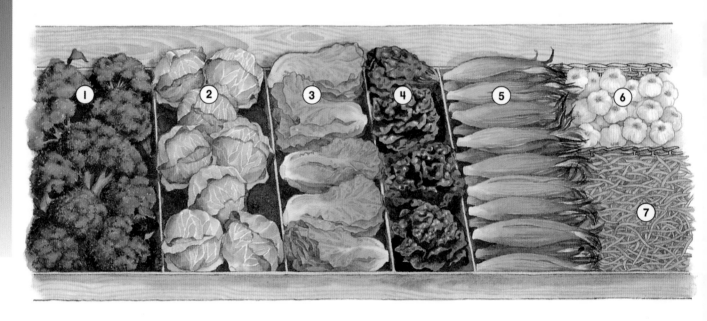

1. broccoli
2. cabbage
3. lettuce
4. spinach
5. corn
6. garlic
7. string beans
8. tomato

9. (bell) pepper
10. cucumber
11. potato
12. onion
13. carrot
14. mushrooms
15. peas

Name the vegetables. Point.

Here's the broccoli.
Here are the string beans.

Talk about yourself.

What vegetables do you like?
What vegetables don't you like?

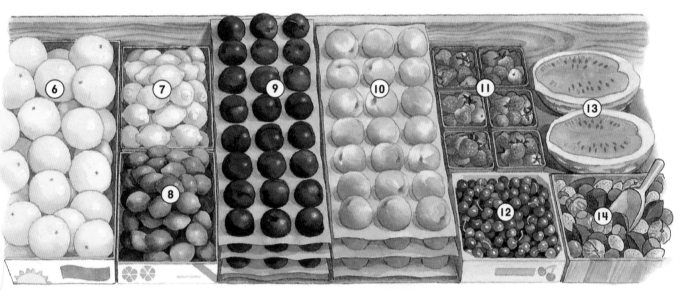

1. bananas
2. grapes
3. apples
4. oranges
5. pears
6. grapefruit
7. lemons

8. limes
9. plums
10. peaches
11. strawberries
12. cherries
13. watermelons
14. nuts

the same

Name the fruits in the green basket.
Count the fruits in pictures 6, 9–10.

There are _____ grapefruit, _____ plums, and
_____ peaches.

Talk about yourself.

A: Do you like <u>bananas</u>?
B: Yes, I do. / No, I don't.

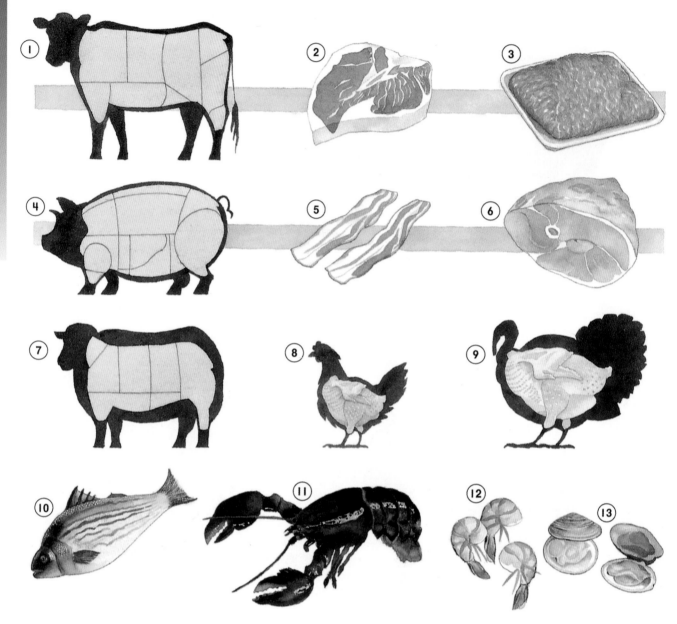

1. beef
2. steak
3. ground meat
4. pork
5. bacon
6. ham
7. lamb

8. chicken
9. turkey
10. fish
11. lobster
12. shrimp
13. clams

Name the meat or seafood. Point.

This is <u>beef</u>.
These are <u>clams</u>.

Talk about yourself.

I eat _____ and _____.
I don't eat _____ and _____.

1. a carton of milk
2. a container of yogurt
3. a bottle of soda
4. a package of cookies
5. a loaf of bread
6. a bag of flour

7. a jar of coffee
8. a can of soup
9. a roll of toilet paper
10. a box of cereal
11. a bar of soap
12. a tube of toothpaste

Name the pictures. Point.

This is a carton of milk.

Language note:

1 carton	2 cartons
1 loaf	2 loaves
1 box	2 boxes

Talk about shopping for food.

A: *What do you need from the store?*
B: *A can of soup, two loaves of bread, and two boxes of cereal.*

1. milk
2. cream
3. sugar
4. eggs
5. cheese
6. butter
7. margarine

8. yogurt
9. bread
10. cereal
11. coffee
12. tea
13. flour
14. oil

Talk about the food.
• Name the things you can drink.
• Name the things you can eat.
• Name the things you can put on food.

Talk about yourself.
A: *What do you like to drink?*
B: *Milk.*
A: *What do you like to eat?*
B: *Cheese.*

15. rice
16. (dried) beans
17. pasta/noodles
18. soup
19. soda/pop
20. juice

21. cookies
22. salt
23. pepper
24. mustard
25. ketchup
26. mayonnaise

Talk about shopping for food.

A: *What can I get you from the store?*
B: *Rice, sugar, and oil, thanks.*

1. shelf
2. aisle
3. shopping basket
4. shopping cart
5. customer
6. checker / checkout person

7. scale
8. cash register
9. checkout (counter)
10. groceries
11. bag
12. packer / bagger
13. bottle return

Name the things in the supermarket. Point.

This is a shelf.
This is an aisle.
These are groceries.

A: Ask questions and point.
B: Answer.

A: *Does he work here?*
B: *Yes, he does. He's a packer.*
   No, he doesn't. He's a customer.

EXPRESS LANE

RECYCLE

A. push

B. carry

C. pay for

D. choose / pick out

E. put in

F. take out

G. weigh

H. pack

Language note:

push → pushing

put in → putting in

take out → taking out

Talk about the picture. Point.

He's *packing groceries*.

She's *carrying a bag*.

A: Ask the question. Act it out.

B: Guess.

A: *What am I doing?*

B: *You're pushing a shopping cart.*

1. table
2. silverware
3. place mat
4. bowl
5. plate
6. glass
7. cup

8. saucer
9. salt and pepper shakers
10. napkin
11. fork
12. knife
13. spoon

Language note:

1 place mat	2 place mats
1 glass	2 glasses
1 knife	2 knives

silverware = forks, knives, spoons

Talk about the picture.
Ask and answer questions about items 3–13.
A: How many <u>place mats</u> are there?
B: <u>Four.</u>

Talk about yourself.

I use _____, _____, and _____ on my table.

1. cook	7. waitress
2. dishwasher	8. menu
3. booth	9. high chair
4. water	10. smoking section
5. busboy	11. no smoking section
6. waiter	12. cashier

Talk about the restaurant.

A: Ask questions and point.

B: Answer.

A: *Who's this?*

B: *A cook.*

A: *What's this?*

B: *A booth.*

Common Prepared Foods

1. scrambled eggs
2. sausage
3. fried eggs
4. toast
5. muffin / English muffin
6. waffles
7. pancakes

8. syrup
9. donuts
10. sandwich
11. hamburger
12. french fries
13. hot dog

Talk about the food.
- **Name three foods you like to eat for breakfast.**
- **Name three foods you like to eat for lunch.**
- **Name three foods you like to eat for dinner.**

Talk about yourself.
A: *What do you eat for <u>breakfast</u>?*
B: *I eat <u>scrambled eggs</u> and <u>a muffin</u>.*

Dinner

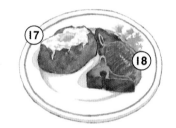

Dessert

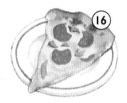

14. salad
15. spaghetti
16. pizza
17. baked potato
18. pork chop

19. mashed potatoes
20. fried chicken
21. ice cream
22. apple pie

Talk about ordering in a restaurant.

A: *What can I get you?*
B: *I'll have <u>a sandwich</u>, <u>french fries</u>, and <u>ice cream</u>, please.*

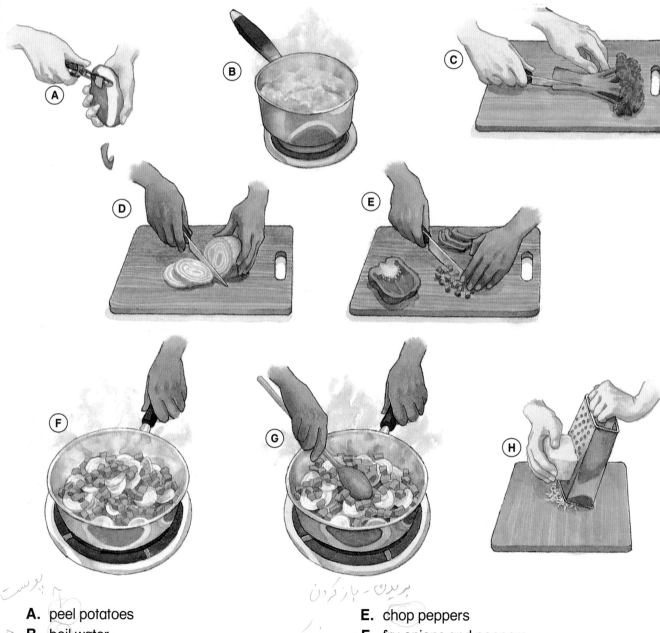

A. peel potatoes
B. boil water
C. cut broccoli
D. slice onions

E. chop peppers
F. fry onions and peppers
G. stir onions and peppers
H. grate cheese

Language note:

peel → peeling
cut → cutting
slice → slicing

Talk about the pictures. Point.

She's peeling potatoes.

A: Ask the question. Act it out.
B: Guess.

A: What am I doing?
B: You're chopping something.

I. steam vegetables
J. pour milk
K. mix ingredients

L. bake a casserole
M. broil fish

Use the new words with pages 34–35.
Ask and answer questions.

A: *What foods do you steam?*
B: *I steam carrots.*

Language note:

First, slice onions.
Then, chop peppers.
Next, fry onions and peppers.

Talk about preparing a food you like.

I like to make _____.
First, grate cheese.

1. dress
2. blouse
3. skirt
4. shirt
5. tie
6. belt

7. pants
8. shoe
9. suit
10. cap
11. uniform

Talk about the people. Point.

She's wearing a dress.
He's wearing pants and shoes.

Talk about yourself.

I'm wearing _____ and _____.

1. swimtrunks / bathing suit	6. baseball cap
2. swimsuit / bathing suit	7. T-shirt
3. sunglasses	8. sneakers / athletic shoes
4. jeans	9. shorts
5. sandals	10. warm-up suit

Talk about the people. Point.

He's wearing a bathing suit.
She's wearing jeans and a T-shirt.
They're wearing athletic shoes.

A: **Ask questions and point.**
B: **Answer.**

A: *What are they wearing?*
B: *Shorts and T-shirts.*
A: *What's she wearing?*
B: *Sunglasses and sandals.*

49

Cold Weather Clothes

1. jacket
2. (down) vest
3. sweater
4. hat → cap
5. sweatshirt
6. backpack
7. boots

8. raincoat
9. umbrella
10. scarf
11. coat
12. mittens
13. gloves
14. earmuffs

Talk about the people.

A: Ask questions.

B: Answer and point.

A: *Who's wearing a jacket?*

B: *He is.*

A: *Who's wearing gloves?*

B: *She is.*

Talk about yourself.

A: *What do you wear in cold weather?*

B: *A coat and gloves.*

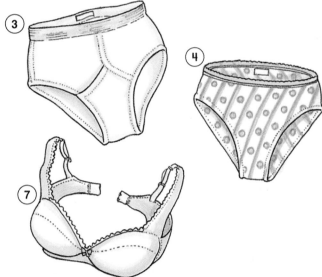

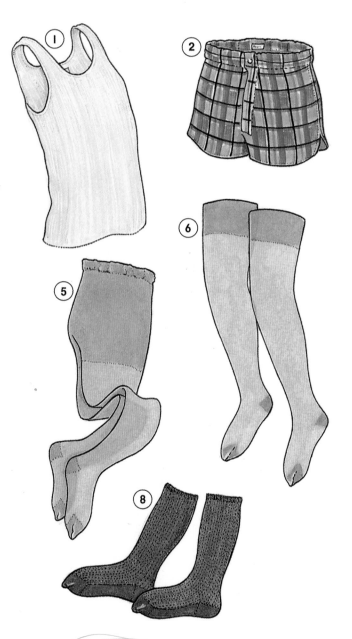

1. undershirt
2. boxer shorts
3. underpants
4. panties
5. pantyhose
6. stockings

7. bra
8. socks
9. nightgown
10. pajamas
11. bathrobe
12. slippers

Talk about the clothes.
• Name the clothes for men.
• Name the clothes for women.
• Name the clothes for men and women.

Language note:
a pair of socks
a pair of slippers
Name five things that come in pairs.

Describing Clothes

1. heavy
2. light
3. new
4. old
5. clean

6. dirty
7. high
8. low
9. narrow
10. wide

Language note:

The opposite of **heavy** is **light.**
The opposite of **narrow** is **wide.**

Look at pictures 1–16.
Ask and answer questions.

A: *What's the opposite of new?*
B: *Old.*

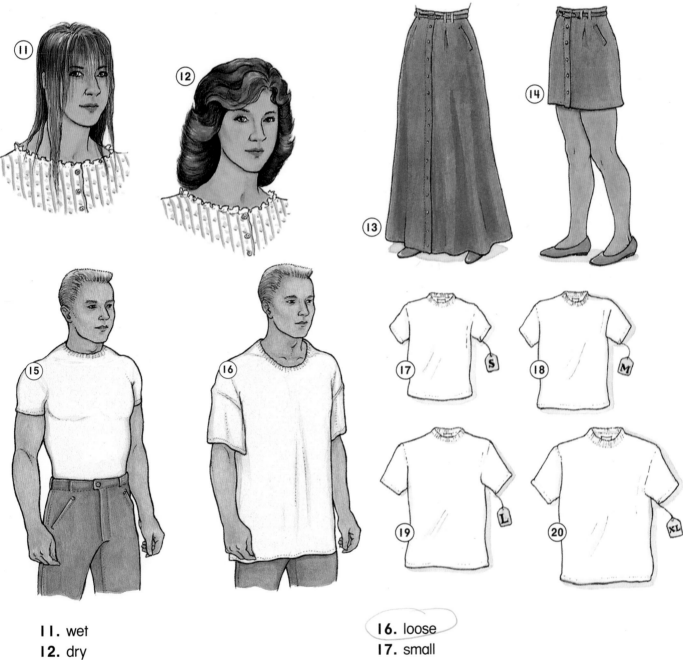

11. wet
12. dry
13. long
14. short
15. tight

16. loose
17. small
18. medium
19. large
20. extra-large

Talk about pictures 11–16. Point.

Her hair is wet.
Her skirt is long.
His shirt is tight.

A: **Ask questions about 17–20 and point.**
B: **Answer.**
A: *What size is that shirt?*
B: *It's a small. / It's an extra-large.*

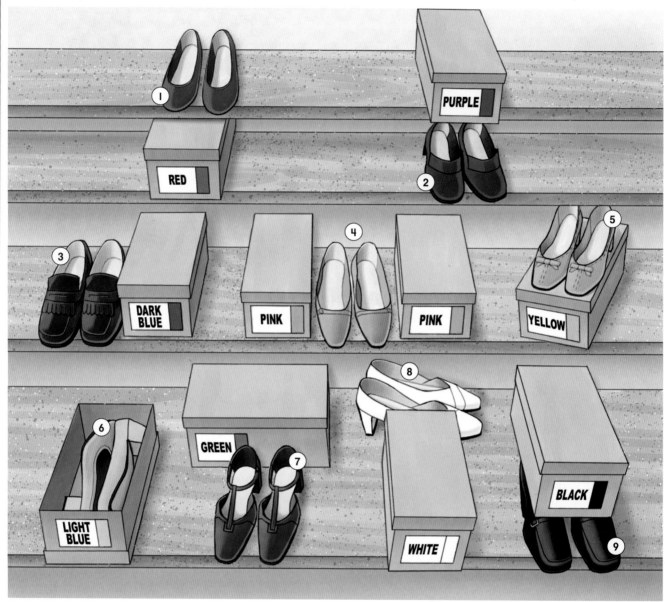

1. above the box	6. in the box
2. below the box	7. in front of the box
3. next to the box	8. behind the box
4. between the boxes	9. under the box
5. on the box	

Talk about the shoes. Point.

The red shoes are above the box.
The white shoes are behind the box.

Ask and answer questions.

A: *Where are the yellow shoes?*
B: *On the box.*

54

1. ring
2. bracelet
3. earrings
4. necklace
5. purse/bag

6. watch
7. change
8. glasses
9. wallet
10. ID card

Talk about the picture. Count.

She has _____ necklaces and _____ bracelets.
She's wearing _____ necklace and
_____ bracelets.

Language note:

I carry a wallet / change / an ID card.
I wear earrings / a ring.

Ask and answer questions.

A: What do you carry with you?
B: A wallet.
A: What do you usually wear?
B: Earrings.

Talk about yourself.

I'm wearing _____ .

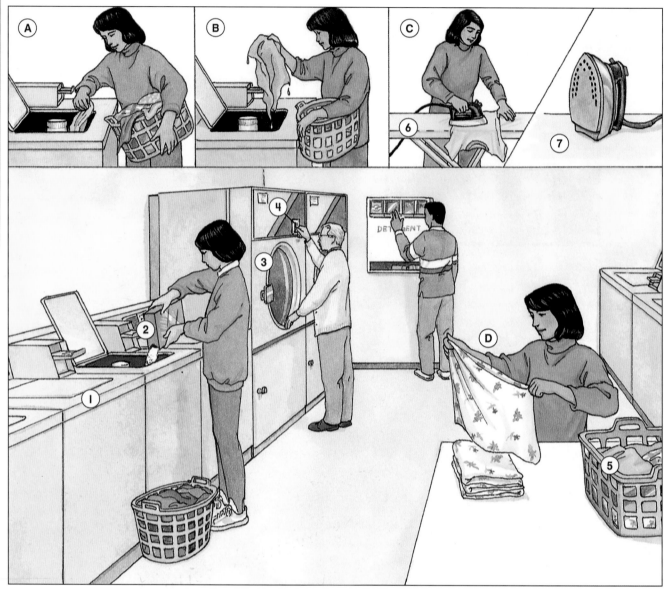

1. washer / washing machine
2. detergent
3. dryer
4. slot
5. laundry basket
6. ironing board
7. iron

A. load / put in
B. unload / take out
C. iron
D. fold

Talk about pictures 1–7.

Here's the washing machine.

A: **Tell your partner what to do.**
B: **Act it out.**

A: *Load the washing machine.*
   Take out the clothes.

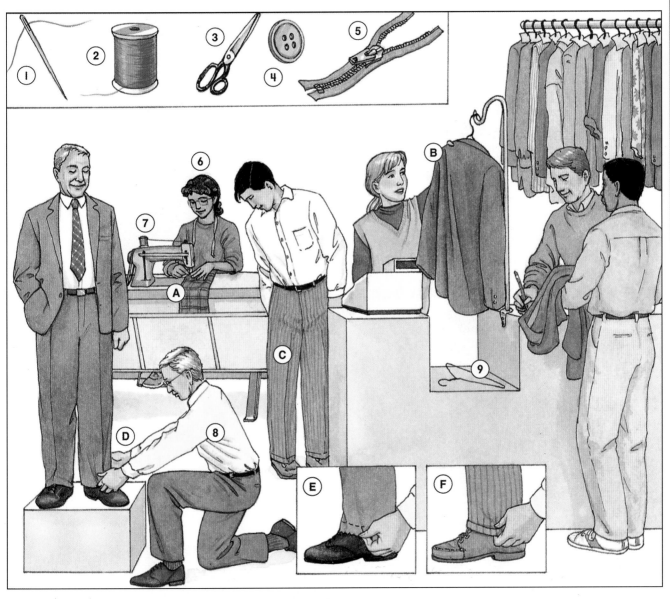

1. needle
2. thread
3. scissors
4. button
5. zipper
6. seamstress
7. sewing machine
8. tailor
9. hanger

A. sew
B. hang up
C. try on
D. alter/do alterations
E. lengthen
F. shorten

Look at pictures 1–9.
- **Name four things for sewing.**
- **Name two people who sew.**

Look at pictures A–F.
A: **Tell your partner what to do.**
B: **Act it out.**

A: *Please <u>sew</u> this jacket.*
  Please <u>hang up</u> this jacket.

1. face
2. neck
3. shoulder
4. chest *medicine chest*
5. hand
6. waist
7. hip

8. finger
9. thumb
10. wrist
11. head
12. arm
13. breast
14. leg

Talk about the pictures.
A: Ask the question and point.
B: Answer.

A: *What's this?*
B: *His face. / Her back.*

15. back
16. thigh
17. elbow
18. knee
19. calf
20. ankle
21. foot

22. heel
23. toe
24. brain
25. lung
26. heart
27. stomach

A: Tell your partner what to do.
Use words 15–23.
B: Act it out.
A: Point to your elbow.

Use the new words with pages 48–49.
Talk about the people. Point.
This is his knee.
This is her shoulder.

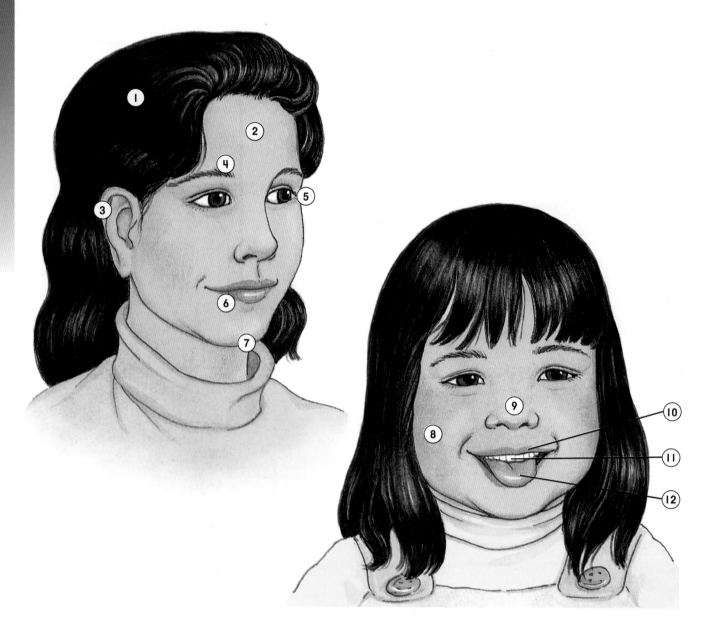

1. hair
2. forehead
3. ear
4. eyebrow
5. eye
6. mouth

7. chin
8. cheek
9. nose
10. lip
11. tooth
12. tongue

Talk about the pictures.

A: Ask the question and point.

B: Answer.

A: What's this?

B: Her hair.

Use the new words with page 24.
Talk about the woman. Point.

This is her forehead.

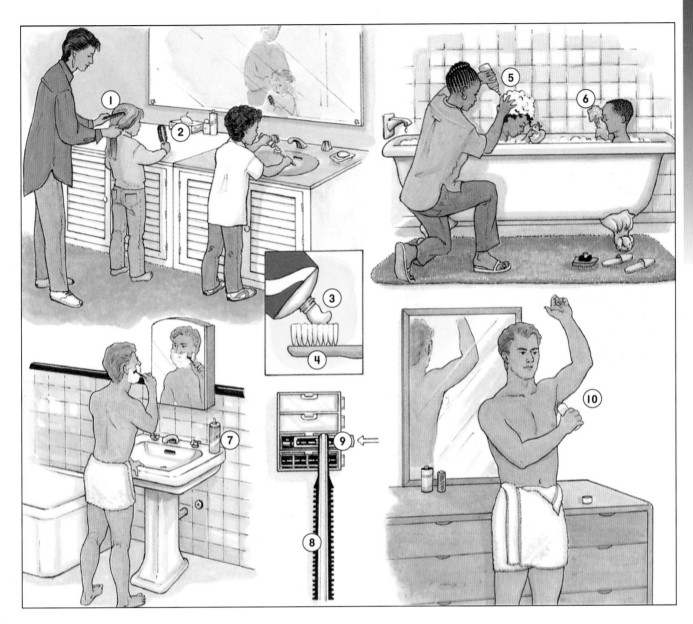

1. comb
2. brush ~~scrub~~
3. toothpaste
4. toothbrush
5. shampoo

6. washcloth
7. shaving cream
8. razor
9. blades
10. deodorant

Talk about the pictures. Point.

She's using a comb.
He's using shaving cream.

A: Ask the question. Act it out.
B: Guess.

A: What am I using?
B: Toothpaste and a toothbrush.

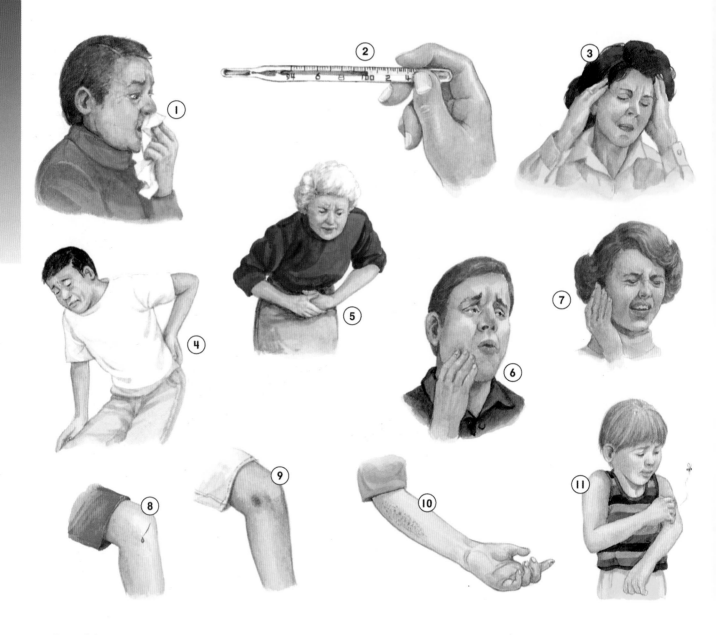

1. cold
2. fever
3. headache
4. backache
5. stomachache
6. toothache

7. earache
8. cut
9. bruise
10. rash
11. insect bite

Talk about pictures 1–17. Point.

He has a cold.
She has an earache.
He has high blood pressure.

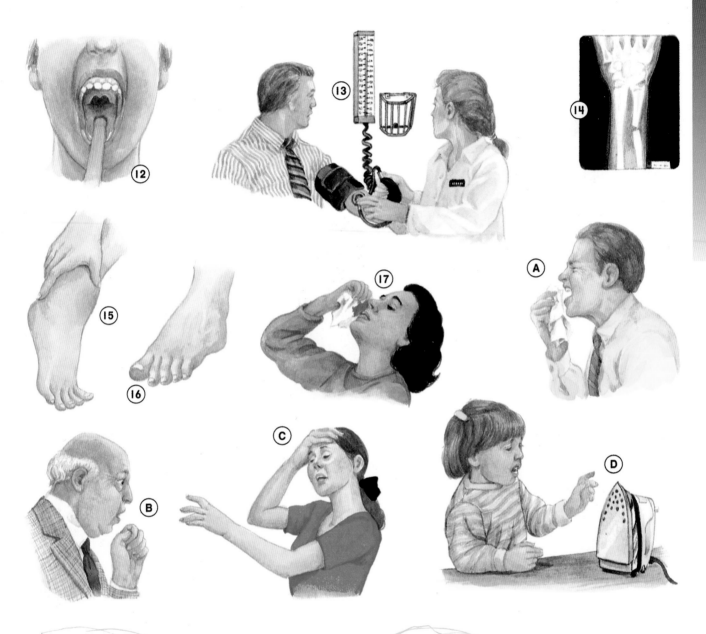

12. sore throat
13. high blood pressure
14. broken arm
15. swollen ankle
16. infected toe
17. bloody nose

A. sneeze
B. cough
C. faint
D. burn . . . self

A: **Ask the question and point.**
B: **Answer.**

A: *What's the matter?*
B: *She has a headache.*

Talk about pictures A–C.

He's going to sneeze.

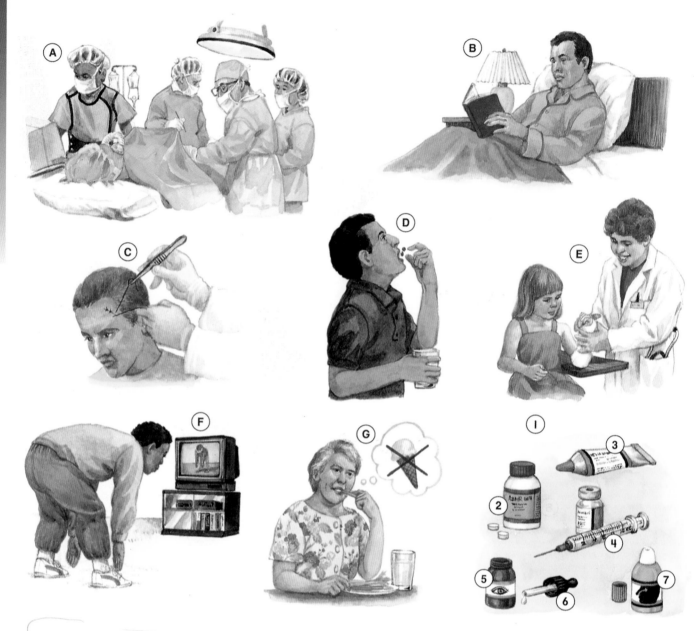

A. have an operation

B. get rest

C. get stitches

D. take medicine

E. get a cast

F. exercise

G. diet

1. medicine / drugs

2. pills

3. cream / ointment

4. injection / shot

5. drops

6. medicine dropper

7. spray

Language note:

have → having

get → getting

Talk about pictures A–G. Point.

She's *having an operation*.

He's *getting rest*.

A: Ask questions about 1–7.

B: Answer and point.

A: *Where are the pills?*

B: *Here they are.*

A: *Where's the cream?*

B: *Here it is.*

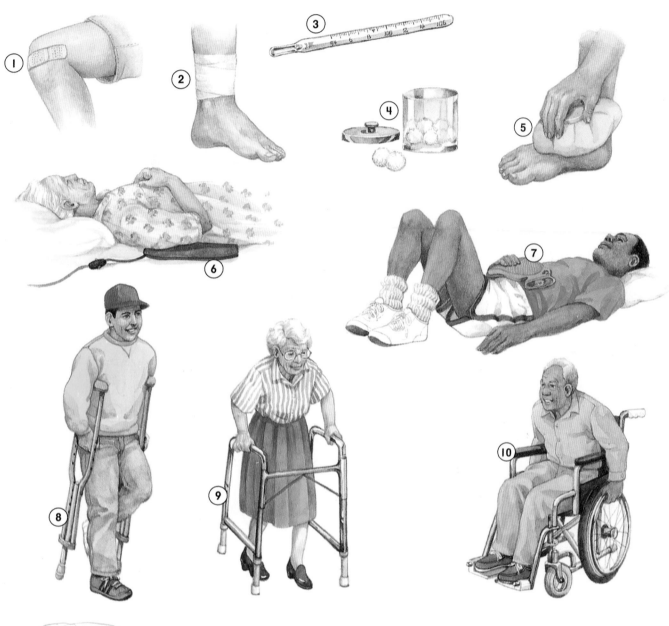

1. Band-Aid
2. bandage
3. thermometer
4. cotton balls
5. ice pack

6. heating pad
7. hot water bottle
8. crutches
9. walker
10. wheelchair

Name the items. Point.

This is a Band-Aid.
This is an ice pack.
These are cotton balls.

Use the new words with pages 62–63.
Talk about the people. Point.

He needs a heating pad.
She needs a Band-Aid.

1. waiting room
2. receptionist
3. insurance form
4. insurance card
5. patient

6. doctor
7. nurse
8. examining room
9. X ray
10. prescription

Talk about the pictures. Count.

There are _____ patients in the waiting room.
There are _____ medical workers.

Look at pictures 1–10.
A: Ask questions and point.
B: Answer.

A: *Who's* <u>*she*</u>?
B: *The receptionist.*
A: *What's this?*
B: *An X ray.*

66

A. fill out the form

B. print name

C. sign name

D. show insurance card

E. wait

F. examine the patient

G. weigh the patient

H. take . . . temperature

I. give a shot / an injection

J. write a prescription

Talk about the patient in pictures A–D.

First, she fills out the form.

Then, she _____ .

Next, she _____ .

Look at pictures F–J.
Ask and answer questions.

A: What does the doctor do?

B: She examines the patient.

A: What does the nurse do?

B: She takes his temperature.

67

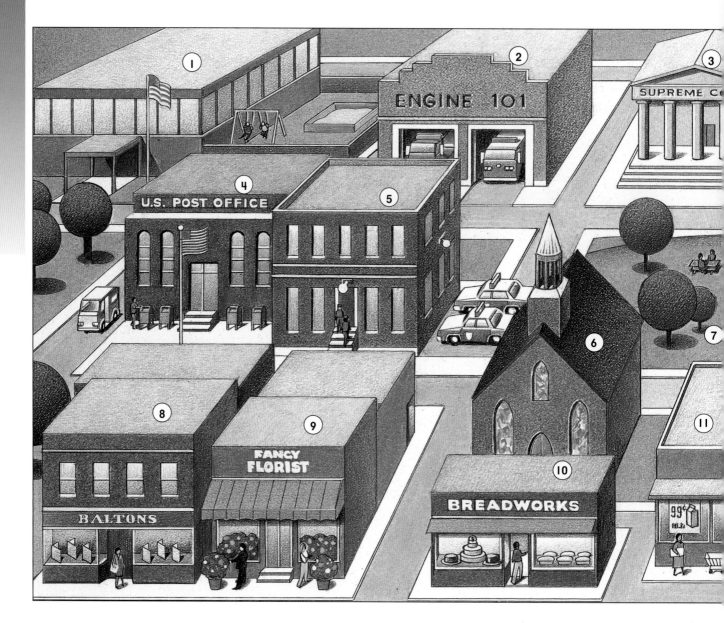

1. school	7. park
2. firehouse	8. bookstore
3. courthouse	9. florist
4. post office	10. bakery
5. police station	11. supermarket
6. church	

Talk about the picture. Point.

This is the school.

Language note:

*The bookstore is **next to** the florist.*
*The city hall is **across from** the park.*
*The school is **near** the post office.*

Ask and answer the questions.

A: *Where's the parking garage?*
B: *It's near the park.*
A: *Where's the post office?*
B: *It's next to the police station.*

12. city hall
13. bus station
14. train station
15. parking garage
16. Department of Motor Vehicles (DMV)

17. office building
18. movie theater
19. mall
20. department store
21. parking lot

Ask and answer questions about your community.

A: Is there *a mall* nearby?
B: Yes, there is.
A: Is there *a train station*?
B: No, there isn't.

Talk about your community.
Name five places you go.

I go to _____, _____, _____, _____,
and _____ .

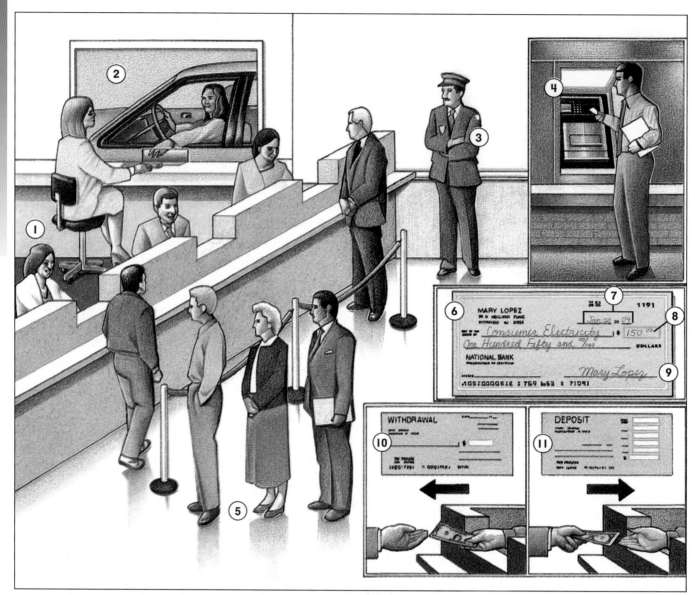

1. teller
2. drive-thru window
3. security guard
4. ATM/cash machine
5. line
6. check

7. date
8. amount
9. signature
10. withdrawal slip
11. deposit slip

Talk about pictures 1–6, 10, 11. Point.

She's a teller.
This is a drive-thru window.

Name three things you can write on a check.

Talk about yourself.

A: *Do you use an ATM?*
B: *Yes, I do. / No, I don't.*
A: *Do you write checks?*
B: *Yes, I do. / No, I don't.*

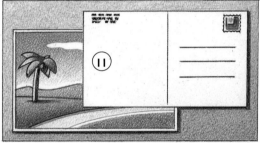

MONICA FUENTES
384 W. 190th ST.
APT. 3J
NEW YORK NY 10040

JOE FERNANDEZ
343 CARMELITA DRIVE
LOS ANGELES, CA 94120

POSTAL MONEY ORDER

33381703381   60126   19002   *45 *19

PAY TO

◄0010812►   355084906

1. postal worker /
   postal clerk
2. package
3. letter carrier
4. mailbox
5. letter
6. envelope

7. return address
8. stamp
9. address
10. zip code
11. postcard
12. money order

Talk about pictures 1–6, 11, 12. Point.
He's a postal clerk.
This is a package.

Talk about an envelope.
Use words 7–10. Point.
Put the return address here.

1. traffic light
2. pedestrian
3. crosswalk
4. public telephone
5. corner
6. intersection

7. newsstand
8. parking meter
9. sidewalk
10. curb
11. bus stop
12. bench

Talk about the picture. Count.

There are _____ traffic lights.
There are _____ pedestrians.
There are _____ people at the bus stop.

A: Ask questions.
B: Answer and point.

A: Where's the newsstand?
B: Here it is.
A: Where are the parking meters?
B: Here they are.

A. come out of the store	**G.** buy groceries
B. go into the store	**H.** look at the windows/clothes
C. make a phone call	**I.** walk
D. stop	**J.** turn
E. cross the street	**K.** wait for the bus
F. mail a letter	

Language note:

come → *coming*
stop → *stopping*
walk → *walking*

Talk about the picture. Point.

She's coming out of the store.
The bus is stopping.

A: Ask questions.
B: Answer and point.

A: *Who's crossing the street?*
B: *He is.*
A: *Who's mailing a letter?*
B: *She is.*

1. smoke	8. police officer
2. fire	9. mugging
3. fire fighter	10. flood
4. accident	11. earthquake
5. ambulance	12. tornado
6. paramedic	13. hurricane
7. robbery / theft	

Talk about the pictures.

• **Count the emergency workers.**

• **Name them.**

A: Ask questions about the pictures. Point.

B: Answer.

A: *What happened?*

B: *There was a fire.*
   There was an earthquake.

A. fall (down)

B. have a heart attack

C. drown

D. swallow poison

E. choke

Language note:

fall → falling

have → having

drown → drowning

A: Ask questions about pictures A–E. Point.

B: Answer.

A: *What's the emergency?*

B: *She's falling.*

1. car
2. bus
3. truck
4. van
5. motorcycle
6. taxi(cab) / cab

7. subway
8. plane
9. train
10. ship
11. bicycle

Talk about the pictures.
A: Ask the question and point.
B: Answer.
A: *What's this?*
B: *A car.*

Talk about yourself.
A: *How do you get to school?*
B: *By bus.*
A: *How do you like to travel?*
B: *By train.*

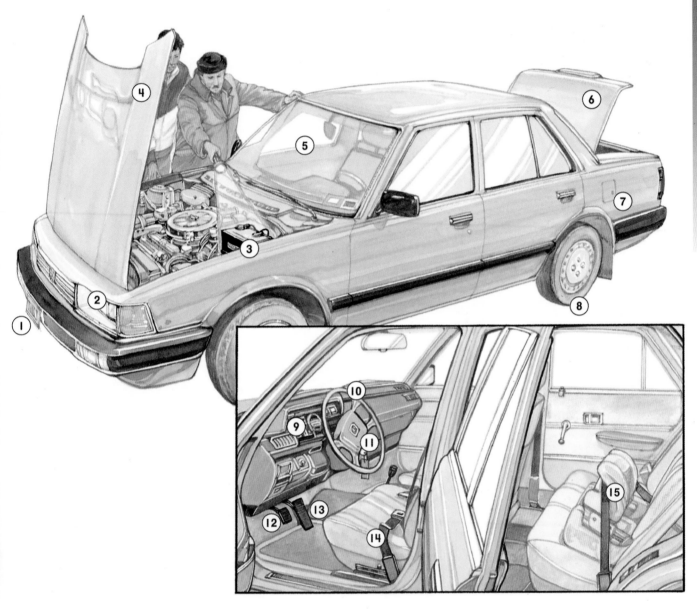

1. license plate
2. headlights
3. battery
4. hood
5. windshield
6. trunk
7. gas tank
8. tire

9. dashboard
10. steering wheel
11. ignition
12. brake
13. accelerator / gas pedal
14. seat belt
15. car seat

Talk about the car.
• **Name three things inside the car.**
• **Name three things on the outside of the car.**
• **Name three things the driver uses.**

Ask and answer questions.
A: *Where's the license plate?*
B: *Here it is.*
A: *Where are the headlights?*
B: *Here they are.*

1. over the highway
2. to / toward the city

3. away from the city
4. through the tunnel

Talk about the picture. Point.

The gray car is going over the highway.
The blue car is going away from the city.

Ask and answer questions.

A: *Is the red car going toward the city?*
B: *Yes, it is. / No, it isn't.*

5. down the hill
6. up the hill
7. across the traffic

8. into the gas station
9. out of the gas station
10. around the accident

Ask and answer questions.

A: *Where's the <u>purple</u> car going?*
B: *<u>Up the hill</u>.*

Ask and answer questions. Use pictures 2, 3, 5, 6, 8, 9.

A: *Is the <u>green</u> car going <u>up the hill</u> or <u>down the hill</u>?*
B: *<u>Down the hill</u>.*

1. passenger
2. ticket
3. suitcase/luggage
4. security check
5. boarding pass

6. gate
7. flight attendant
8. pilot
9. baggage claim

Talk about the pictures. Count.

There are _____ passengers.
There are _____ tickets.
There are _____ suitcases.

A: Ask questions about 4–9.
B: Answer and point.

A: *Where's the security check?*
B: *Here it is.*
A: *Where's the flight attendant?*
B: *Here she is.*

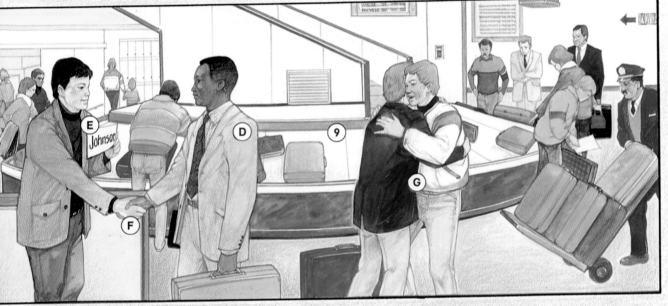

A. check bags

B. leave/depart

C. wave (good-bye)

D. arrive

E. meet

F. shake hands

G. hug

Language note:

check	→	checking
leave	→	leaving
hug	→	hugging

Talk about A–G. Point.

He's checking bags.

They're leaving.

1. pharmacist / druggist
2. drugstore
3. mechanic
4. attendant
5. service station /
   gas station

6. butcher
7. butcher shop
8. hairdresser / hairstylist
9. beauty salon
10. barber
11. barbershop

Talk about the pictures.
- **Name the people who work outdoors.**
- **Name the people who work indoors.**
- **Name the people who work indoors and outdoors.**

Talk about the pictures. Point.

She's a pharmacist. She works in a drugstore.
He's a mechanic. He works in a service station.

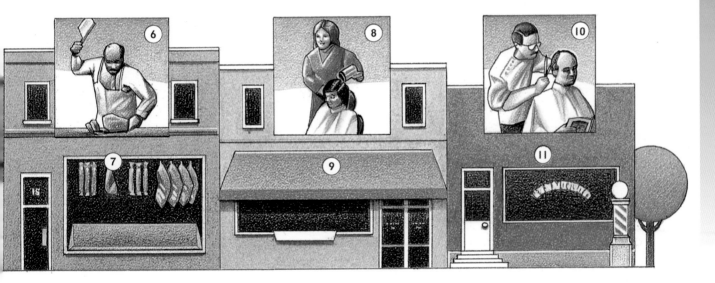

12. librarian
13. library
14. dentist
15. dental assistant
16. office

17. grocer
18. fruit and vegetable market
19. sanitation worker
20. delivery person

Look at pictures 1–18.
Ask and answer questions.

A: *Where does a dentist work?*
B: *In an office.*

Talk about yourself.

A: *Would you like to be a barber?*
B: *Yes, I would. / No, I wouldn't.*

1. plumber
2. electrician
3. locksmith
4. housekeeper
5. gardener
6. painter
7. construction worker

8. janitor / custodian
9. mover
10. superintendent /
    apartment manager
11. doorman
12. taxi driver

Talk about the pictures.
- **Name the workers who wear a uniform.**
- **Name the workers who work outdoors.**
- **Name the workers who work indoors.**
- **Name the workers who drive at work.**

84

13. factory worker
14. foreman
15. bus driver
16. carpenter
17. maintenance man
18. fisherman

19. truck driver
20. farmer
21. soldier
22. sewing machine operator
23. (train) conductor

A: Ask questions and point.
B: Answer.

A: *What does he do?*
B: *He's a factory worker.*

Talk about yourself.

A: *Would you like to be an electrician?*
B: *Yes, I would. / No, I wouldn't.*

1. secretary
2. typist / word processor
3. file clerk
4. computer programmer
5. messenger
6. photographer
7. reporter
8. businessman / businesswoman

9. accountant
10. lawyer
11. salesperson
12. babysitter
13. dancer
14. singer
15. actor / actress
16. artist

Talk about the pictures.
- **Count the office workers.**
- **Name them.**

A: Ask questions and point.
B: Answer.

A: *What does she do?*
B: *She's a singer. / She's an actress.*

A. take out

B. put in

C. dig

D. oversee

E. lay

F. pour

G. measure

H. hammer

I. climb

J. scrape

K. paint

Language note:

take out / put in a window
dig a hole
oversee the work
lay bricks
pour cement

Look at the pictures.

A: Tell your partner what to do.

B: Act it out.

A: *Take out a window.*
   Measure something.

A. fix / repair TVs / appliances
B. fix / repair cars
C. fix / repair pipes
D. cut hair
E. cut meat
F. cut grass

G. sell clothes
H. sell vegetables
I. sell newspapers
J. build houses
K. build furniture

Talk about the pictures.
• Name three things you can fix.
• Name three things you can cut.
• Name three things you can sell.

• Name three things you can drive.
• Name three things you can deliver.

مراقبت مهواظبت

L. take care of children

M. take care of pools

N. take care of grounds

O. drive a bus

P. drive a cab   تاکسی

Q. drive a truck

رساندن - تحویل

R. deliver mail

خوار بار فروشی

S. deliver groceries

بسته بندی

T. deliver packages

U. collect garbage

جمع کردن - گرد آوردن

V. collect fares   زباله

W. collect tickets

Language note:

He fixes cars.

She sells clothes.

She takes care of children.

A: **Ask questions and point.**

B: **Answer.**

A: *What does he do?*

B: *He takes care of pools.*

A Day-Care Center

1. day-care worker / child-care worker
2. stroller
3. pacifier
4. bottle
5. nipple
6. diaper

7. toy
8. bib
9. playpen
10. crib
11. rattle
12. cradle

Talk about the picture. Count.

There are _____ day-care workers.

Name three things for babies.

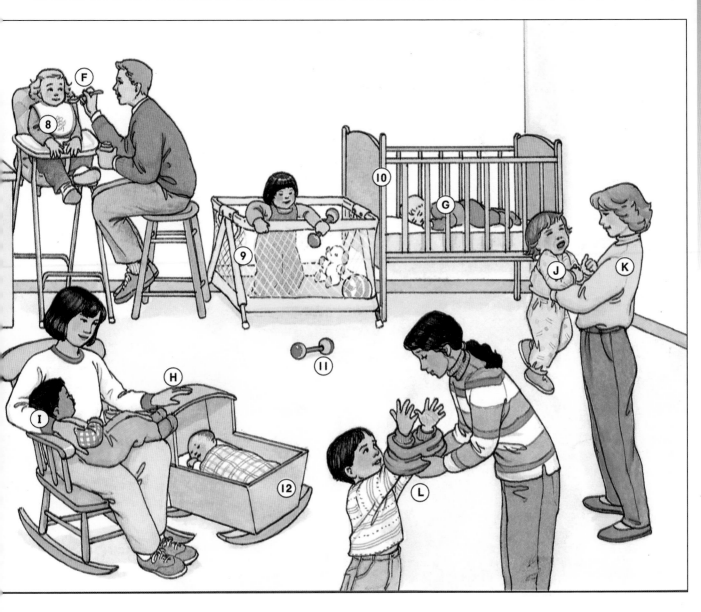

A. bring/drop off	**G.** take a nap
B. change diapers	**H.** rock
C. play	**I.** hold
D. crawl	**J.** cry
E. run	**K.** pick up
F. feed	**L.** dress

Language note:

drop off	→	dropping off
change	→	changing
cry	→	crying

A: Ask questions.
B: Answer and point.

A: Who's <u>crying</u>?
B: <u>She</u> is.
A: Who's <u>feeding</u> the baby?
B: <u>He</u> is.

Leisure

Outdoor Activities

A. go camping

B. go hiking

Sports

C. play tennis

D. play football

E. play basketball

F. play soccer

G. play baseball

H. go skiing

Talk about the pictures.

• Name activities you can do outdoors.

• Name activities you can do indoors.

Talk about yourself.

A: *What sports do you play?*

B: *I play baseball. / I don't play any sports.*

Indoor Activities آلت موسیقی
موسیقی
- **I.** play an instrument
- **J.** go to the movies
- **K.** watch TV
- **L.** listen to music

Exercise
- **M.** go swimming
- **N.** go running

Talk about yourself.

A: *What do you like to do?*

B: *I like to listen to music.*

94

New Year's Eve
A. drink champagne
B. make a toast

Valentine's Day
C. give valentines
D. get flowers

Easter عید پاک
E. paint Easter eggs شکار تخم
F. go on an Easter egg hunt

Memorial Day
G. wave a flag نظام - رژه پیدا یی
H. watch a parade
I. visit a cemetery قبرستان

Name the holidays. Point.

New Year's Eve
the Fourth of July

Ask and answer questions.

A: When do you *make a toast*?
B: On *New Year's Eve*.

Fourth of July

J. have a barbecue / picnic

K. watch fireworks

Halloween

L. carve out a pumpkin

M. wear a costume

N. go trick-or-treating

Thanksgiving

O. get together with family and friends

P. give thanks

Q. eat a big meal

Christmas

R. send cards

S. go Christmas shopping

T. decorate the tree

Talk about yourself.

When do you get together with family and friends?
When do you send cards?

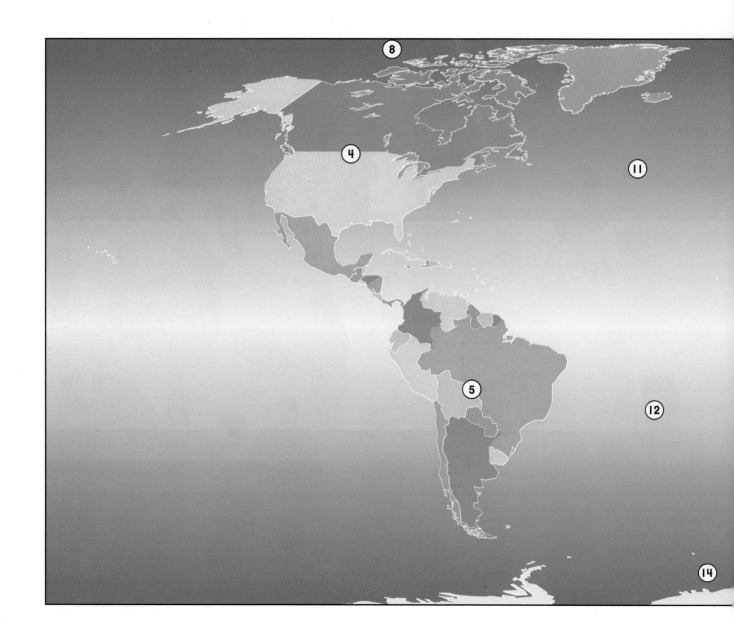

Continents

1. Asia
2. Africa
3. Europe
4. North America
5. South America
6. Australia
7. Antarctica

Oceans

8. Arctic
9. North Pacific
10. South Pacific
11. North Atlantic
12. South Atlantic
13. Indian
14. Antarctic

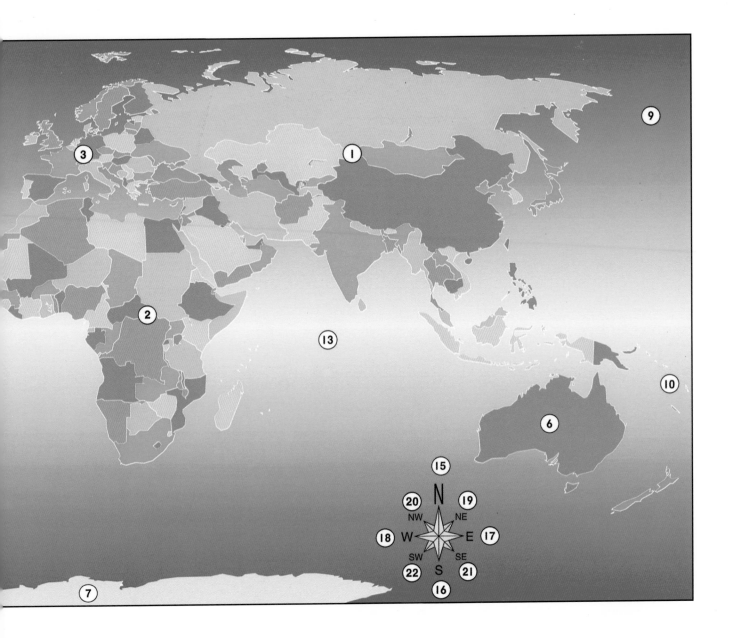

Directions

15. north

16. south

17. east

18. west

19. northeast

20. northwest

21. southeast

22. southwest

1	one	1st	first
2	two	2nd	second
3	three	3rd	third
4	four	4th	fourth
5	five	5th	fifth
6	six	6th	sixth
7	seven	7th	seventh
8	eight	8th	eighth
9	nine	9th	ninth
10	ten	10th	tenth
11	eleven		
12	twelve		
13	thirteen		
14	fourteen		
15	fifteen		
16	sixteen		
17	seventeen		
18	eighteen		
19	nineteen		
20	twenty		
21	twenty-one		
30	thirty		
40	forty		
50	fifty		
60	sixty		
70	seventy		
80	eighty		
90	ninety		
100	a/one hundred		
500	five hundred		
621	six hundred (and) twenty-one		
1,000	a/one thousand		
1,000,000	a/one million		

Abbreviations

ounces	oz
teaspoon	tsp
tablespoon	tbs
pint	pt
quart	qt
gallon	gal
pound(s)	lb(s)
inch	in
foot/feet	ft
yard(s)	yd(s)
mile	mi

liter	l
milliliter	ml
gram	g
milligram	mg
kilogram	kg
meter	m
centimeter	cm
kilometer	km

Length, Height, and Distance

ruler

yardstick

measuring tape

1 ft	12 in
1 yd	3 ft
1 mi	1,760 yds

1 in	2.54 cm
1 ft	30.48 cm
1 yd	.941 m
1 mi	1.609 km

Liquid Measure

teaspoon

tablespoon

cup

a quarter cup

a third of a cup

a half cup

1 oz	29.6 ml
1 c	236.5 ml
1 pt	473 ml
1 qt	.946 l
1/2 gal	1.893 l
1 gal	3.786 l

1 tbs	3 tsp	1/2 oz
1 c	16 tbs	8 oz
1 pt	2 c	16 oz
1 qt	2 pt	32 oz
1/2 gal	2 qt	64 oz
1 gal	4 qt	128 oz

Solid Weights

1 lb	454 g
1 kg	2.205 lbs

Abbreviations

degrees Fahrenheit	°F
degrees Celsius/centigrade	°C

From Fahrenheit to Celsius/Centigrade

subtract 32, multiply by 5, divide by 9

50°F   50
        -32
          18 × 5 = 90

        90 ÷ 9 = 10°C

From Celsius/Centigrade to Fahrenheit

multiply by 9, divide by 5, add 32

10°C   10 × 9 = 90

        90 ÷ 5 = 18
               +32
                 50°F

Two numbers occur after words in the index: the first refers to the page where the word is illustrated and the second to the item number of the word on that page. For example, above [ə bŭv**ʹ**] **54**/1 means that the word *above* is the item numbered 1 on page 54. If only a bold number appears, then that word is part of the unit title or a subtitle.

The index includes a pronunciation guide for all the words illustrated in the book. This guide uses symbols commonly found in dictionaries for native speakers. These symbols, unlike those used in transcription systems such as the International Phonetic Alphabet, tend to preserve spelling and so should help you to become more aware of the connections between written English and spoken English.

Consonants

[b] as in **back** [băk]   [k] as in **kiss** [kĭs]   [sh] as in **ship** [shĭp]
[ch] as in **cheek** [chēk]   [l] as in **leg** [lĕg]   [t] as in **tape** [tāp]
[d] as in **date** [dāt]   [m] as in **man** [măn]   [th] as in **three** [thrē]
[dh] as in **the** [dh]   [n] as in **neck** [nĕk]   [v] as in **vest** [vĕst]
[f] as in **face** [fās]   [ng] as in **ring** [rĭng]   [w] as in **waist** [wāst]
[g] as in **gas** [găs]   [p] as in **pack** [păk]   [y] as in **yard** [yärd]
[h] as in **half** [hăf]   [r] as in **rake** [rāk]   [z] as in **zip** [zĭp]
[j] as in **jeans** [jēnz]   [s] as in **sad** [săd]   [zh] as in **measure** [mĕzh**ʹ**ər]

Vowels

[ā] as in **bake** [bāk]   [ī] as in **lime** [līm]   [o͞o] as in **cool** [ko͞ol]
[ă] as in **back** [băk]   [ĭ] as in **lip** [lĭp]   [o͝o] as in **book** [bo͝ok]
[ä] as in **bar** [bär]   [ï] as in **heel** [hïl]   [ow] as in **brown** [brown]
[ē] as in **bean** [bēn]   [ō] as in **post** [pōst]   [oy] as in **boy** [boy]
[ĕ] as in **bed** [bĕd]   [ŏ] as in **box** [bŏks]   [ŭ] as in **cut** [kŭt]
[ë] as in **pear** [për]   [ö] as in **lawn** [lön]   [ü] as in **curb** [kürb]
                                          or **for** [för]   [ə] as in **above** [ə bŭv**ʹ**]

All pronunciation symbols used are alphabetical except for the schwa [ə], which is the most frequent vowel sound in English. If you use it appropriately in unstressed syllables, your pronunciation will sound more natural.

You should note that an umlaut ([¨]) calls attention to the special quality of vowels before [r]. (The sound [ö] can also represent a vowel not followed by [r] as in *lawn*.) You should listen carefully to native speakers to discover how these vowels actually sound.

Stress

This guide also follows the system for marking stress used in many dictionaries for native speakers.
   (1) Stress is not marked if a word consisting of a single syllable occurs in isolation.
   (2) Where stress is marked, two levels are distinguished:
       a bold accent [**ʹ**] is placed after each syllable with primary stress.
       a light accent [ʹ] is placed after each syllable with secondary stress.

Syllable Boundaries

Syllable boundaries are indicated by a single space.

NOTE: The pronunciation used in this index is based on patterns of American English. There has been no attempt to represent all of the varieties of American English. Students should listen to native speakers to hear how the language actually sounds in a particular region.

Index

Index

Index